Mysteries
A Journey Around the World

By
TEDDY MEISTER

COPYRIGHT © 2005 Mark Twain Media, Inc.

ISBN 1-58037-306-2

Printing No. CD-404033

Mark Twain Media, Inc., Publishers
Distributed by Carson-Dellosa Publishing Company, Inc.

Table of Contents

Introduction

We live in an age of monumental amounts of continuously expanding human knowledge. Technological advances have provided answers to many of yesterday's questions and greater understandings of the world around us. However, mysteries abound that modern science has yet to definitively solve. Conjecture and theory still reign, a most humbling realization. As man continually reaches into greater explorations of space, there are still many places on Earth that need further exploration and understanding.

Mysteries: A Journey Around the World is a collection of some of the strangest enigmas that exist on our planet. They have challenged man's imagination throughout the ages. Many defy explanation. Some, existing for centuries, have yet to be explained. There is evidence to examine, but the why and the how remain elusive.

Mysteries: A Journey Around the World will challenge students to investigate as topics unfold. Each can become a "springboard" to stimulate exploration and research. Students' awareness will be enhanced as they embark on a journey through some of the most incredible things they will ever encounter!

How to Use This Book

Each mystery is self-contained and "ready to go." Flexible for use, they are suitable for group or independent study, library research, curriculum enhancement, or homework enrichment assignments. The multi-disciplinary topics can be used in any order. Students can be given choices according to their interests. As single sheets, they can each be mounted on cards, laminated, and set up in a "Mystery" box for handy year-round use.

Each page is set up according to the following format:

1. **The Mystery** – The subject is briefly summarized and can serve as a motivational introduction to spark student interest.

2. **Musings** – From one to three activities will challenge students to demonstrate their knowledge and understanding of the topic and will require some research.

3. **Mental Mixtures** – This activity is designed to develop higher cognitive processes.

4. **Moving Beyond** – A list of related topics is provided to extend students' interest and expand their knowledge of the mystery.

The mysteries used in this book are all authentic and come from all over the globe. The last page, "Summarizing," will establish a broad look at relationships among many of the mysteries. Students will have an opportunity to reflect and gain a sense of some of the strangest things in our world!

Ale Stones

Atop a 100-foot-high cliff that overlooks the Baltic Sea near Ystad, Sweden, stands Ales Stenar (Ale Stones). It has been called the "Swedish Stonehenge." This oval, ship-like formation dates back to the late Stone Age, 3000–1500 B.C., about 3,500 to 5,000 years ago. It measures 200 feet in length and 60 feet at its widest section. The 58 upright stones have been estimated to weigh about five tons each and were probably brought from places almost 15 miles away. Thought to have been built during the age of the Vikings, stones in this type of formation were used to honor the memory of dead kings. Scientists studying the site made precise measurements and concluded that the ship's bow (front) is aligned exactly to the setting summer solstice sun. The stern (rear) is aligned to the rising sun of the winter solstice. The entire structure could have been an early type of calendar.

MUSINGS

1. How does the Ale Stones formation compare with Stonehenge? Set up a two-column sheet of paper. Head one column "Similarities" and the other "Differences." How many of each can be found?

2. Examine a picture of a Viking ship and notice its outline as if you were looking down on it from above. This will provide an idea of what the Ale Stones site looks like. Construct a diagram of what the interior of a Viking ship might look like.

MENTAL MIXTURES

Solstices seem to have been important times of the year for many ancient people. Write a short paragraph explaining your views and the reasons for your opinions.

MOVING BEYOND

Archaeo-astronomy   Bronze Age   Kivik Tomb

Megalithic Period   Stone Age   Vikings

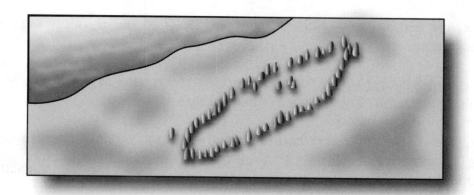

2

America's Stonehenge

An intricate maze-like chamber structure over 4,000 years old is located near Salem, New Hampshire. It is called America's Stonehenge and is probably one of the oldest man-made structures in the United States.

As the site was first explored, archaeologists were intrigued to find a wide assortment of artifacts—stone tools, pottery, stone alignments that seem to be placed in positions to track astronomical movements, and a type of calendar based on certain lunar and solar events during the course of a year. More currently, eighteenth- and nineteenth-century housewares and manacles have also been found on the site. (These are thought to have been used by escaped slaves who stayed there as a refuge during their journey on the Underground Railroad.)

Was this intriguing group of stone structures built by an ancient Native American civilization or a migrant group of people from an area outside this country? Perhaps one day there will be answers rather than questions.

MUSINGS

1. The Underground Railroad was used as an escape route for slaves during the Civil War. Write a brief report about Harriet Tubman and her efforts in aiding slaves to escape from the South.

2. Many ancient cultures were involved in tracking the sun, moon, and stars and creating calendars. Set up a chart showing the ancient groups, i.e., Mayas, Egyptians, Greeks, etc., and the structures that remain that show these ancient calendars. Explain why you think this was important to their cultures.

MENTAL MIXTURES

There are over 350 megalithic sites just in New England. Explore the meaning of this word and identify some of the areas on a map. Is there a pattern? Are they clustered in some way? Be an anthro-archaeologist and present your findings.

MOVING BEYOND

Archaeo-astronomy	Carbon-14 Dating	Eclipses
Epigraphy	Solstices	Telescopes

The Anasazi

Anasazi, the Navajo word for "ancient ones," refers to a prehistoric tribe of Indians who lived in the region known as the "Four Corners." The borders of Utah, Colorado, New Mexico, and Arizona meet at this site. The Anasazi flourished there for hundreds of years. However, more than 2,000 years ago, they disappeared.

Archaeological investigations have shown that they hunted and grew crops. Their homes had brush roofs and were shallow pits dug into the ground. Permanent *pueblos*, or homes, were also built into large openings on the cliff sides, offering natural protection from enemies and from the weather. Many of these were large and several stories high and could hold hundreds of people. Larger areas, or *kivas*, were built for religious ceremonies and communal gatherings.

In recent times, archaeologists observed that in the largest kiva, the sun's rays penetrate a window-like opening and enter niches or shelves around the wall of the main room. During the summer solstice, all 28 niches are aglow with the sunlight at the same time!

The Chaco Canyon dwellings, built around 920 A.D., are the best known. One dwelling that is three stories tall contains 100 rooms. Eleven dwellings that are built in the canyon have a total of 3,000 rooms that held an estimated population of 5,000. The Anasazi also constructed irrigation canals. Over 70 other communities were connected with over 500 miles of roads.

The Anasazi constructions are amazing. Some pueblos using over 30 million stones and more than 100,000 heavy timbers have been explored. Beautiful pottery petroglyphs (markings) and wall paintings are still visible. The Pueblo Indians are present-day descendants of the Anasazi.

MUSINGS

1. Suppose you were assigned the task of leading an archaeological expedition to the Chaco Canyon site. What might be needed for equipment, living facilities, water, and food supplies? What special scientists might also accompany you? Construct an expedition plan.

2. Construct a scale model of a kiva. Find pictures of one of these structures and use natural materials such as twigs, stones, and leaves. Display the finished product in the library or somewhere the whole school can enjoy it.

MENTAL MIXTURES

Some archaeologists have theorized that this ancient society might have brought about its own disappearance. By leveling their forests, using up entire plant and animal species, and exhausting available farmland, the result might have been their extinction. Write a brief paragraph to explain the interdependence of man with the environment.

MOVING BEYOND

| E. Guerrero | Legends | Georgia O'Keeffe |
| Painted Desert | Paleontology | Pueblo Indians |

 # Atlantis—The Lost Continent

Plato first described the lost continent of Atlantis 2,500 years ago. According to him, Atlantis existed 12,000–9,000 B.C. He based this on records kept by Egyptian priests and paintings on temple columns. These columns told a story of Atlantis disappearing as the result of cataclysmic earthquakes and floods. In a single day and night, the entire continent allegedly sank into the ocean without a trace.

Plato wrote detailed descriptions of buildings and technology and the customs and laws of what might have been a very advanced civilization of about 20 million people. Theories have been written about what might have happened. What do you think?

MUSINGS

1. If the Atlanteans had achieved such remarkable technical and scientific skills, it seems plausible that their population may have been warned to leave before the destruction. If you were an Atlantean during this time and had to leave, what items would be important to take for survival? Make a list and provide an explanation of why each item should be taken.

2. "Once upon a time there was beyond the strait you call, 'The Pillars of Hercules,' an island larger than Asia Minor and Libya together ... On this island of Atlantis, there existed a great and admirable kingdom."— Plato in his dialogue *Timaeus*, 350 B.C. Draw a map showing the possible boundaries of Atlantis. Name the geographical borders.

MENTAL MIXTURES

You have been put in charge of an expedition to locate the lost continent of Atlantis. It will be a long and arduous experience. People with special knowledge and skills are to be appointed to join the mission. What types of scientists will be needed? What special equipment is needed for the task? What supplies are necessary? Prepare an "Atlantis Expedition Plan" to present to those financing the journey.

MOVING BEYOND

Ancient Temples	Archaeology/Archaeologists	Artifacts
Early Civilizations	The Pillars of Hercules	Plato

The Bayeux Tapestry

The Bayeux Tapestry is an astonishing work of embroidery that depicts the conquest of Britain as told from the Norman (French) point of view. Created in 1088 for the Bayeux Cathedral of France, it measures about 20 inches wide and stretches *over 230 feet* in length! The entire story of William the Conqueror is told sequentially throughout the embroidered frames. He was victorious over the English forces at the Battle of Hastings in 1066.

Nothing is known of the tapestry's origins. The first written record of it appeared in 1476 where it was simply described as a "very narrow and long hanging on which are embroidered figures and inscriptions comprising a representation of the conquest of England."

Each of about 50 rectangular scenes shows the Battle of Hastings from start to finish. There are over 623 figures in all, 2,000 Latin letters, and more than 700 animals sewn in to tell the story. Also included are ships, buildings, boats, and weapons. The tapestry presents a remarkable pictorial history of the clothing, beliefs, and customs of eleventh-century medieval life.

MUSINGS

1. Find and examine pictures of the tapestry. Notice the style of the ships of the period. Using available materials, construct a model of a Norman ship. Display it in the classroom when completed.

2. The Battle of Hastings was an important event in British and French history. Read about this battle and construct a time line showing the major stages of the battle.

3. The tapestry was embroidered with eight different colored yarns on stiff linen. It is thought to have been sewn by women from a well-known English embroidery school. Learning embroidery was an important skill for young ladies. Investigate other areas of learning for women of the time. Compare the vast differences in the education of young ladies today.

MENTAL MIXTURES

Who was William the Conqueror? What did he do to become famous? Read about his life and times and set up a list of characteristics that would describe him. How do these traits compare with other leaders you have studied?

MOVING BEYOND
Archbishop of Canterbury
Castles
Feudal System
Medieval Queens
Medieval Weapons and Armor
Tapestry Hangings

The Bermuda Triangle

In the western Atlantic Ocean, off the southeast coast of the United States, is an area referred to as the "Graveyard of the Atlantic." One of nature's most perplexing mysteries is the Bermuda Triangle.

This area includes about 440,000 square miles of open sea. It stretches from the tip of south Florida to Puerto Rico and north to Bermuda. Many planes and ships that were traveling through the area seem to have vanished, and more than 1,000 lives have been lost without a trace. One of the most puzzling disappearances was a flight of five Navy Avengers on a mission from Fort Lauderdale, Florida, Naval Air Station on December 5, 1945. All five men and their planes vanished.

Large ships have been lost without explanation, while other ships and boats have been found drifting within the Triangle area without a sign of crew or passengers. Reports from planes and ships before their disappearances have described similar events such as radio, compass, and other instrument malfunctions, yellow and hazy skies, and an ocean that "didn't look right."

There exist ten other regions in the world with similar vanishings. Studied by some of the top mathematicians, geographers, and electromagnetic engineers, the regions seem to be ten equally spaced areas occurring at exactly 72-degree intervals of latitude and longitude. Five are in the Southern Hemisphere, and five are in the Northern Hemisphere. Are they related in some way? Perhaps one day we will know.

MUSINGS

1. Why is the Bermuda Triangle still so mysterious after all the incidents over such a long period of time? What factors make a mystery? Create a short mystery story about this area.

2. Construct a time line of disappearances. Add illustrations and short comments for each.

MENTAL MIXTURES

What do you think is an explanation for the Bermuda Triangle mystery? What might be the cause of the unusual disappearances? Formulate a hypothesis that might explain this mystery.

MOVING BEYOND

Magnetism	Marianas Trench	The *Mary Celeste*
Oceanography	Pacific Ring of Fire	Tidal Waves

Bigfoot

"I was born and raised in this Cascade Mountain area. I know the animals here. This was something different that I had never seen before. I know that it wasn't a bear or some other animal because I know what those animals look like." — *from an eyewitness account*

The Chehalis Indians of British Columbia, Canada, have described this creature as a hairy monster, 7–9 feet in height, and they call it Sasquatch, which means "giant." Enormous footprints, some $14\frac{1}{2}$ to 16 inches in length and 6 to 10 inches in width, confirm reports. The creatures are believed to live in cover in remote mountain areas of the Pacific Northwest. Hundreds of sightings have been reported, and some have even been photographed. Summaries of these suggest that "Bigfoot," or Sasquatch, is a gentle creature who follows the food supply, is quick to sense danger, can move swiftly, and has extraordinary senses of sight, sound, and smell. Many scientists think he might be a survivor of a very early species of ape.

MUSINGS

1. There are many similarities between Bigfoot and the Yeti (Abominable Snowman) of the Himalayas in Tibet. Read about the Yeti, and then set up a chart to compare the two in size, habitats, food sources, and environment.

2. Examine the map locations of these two creatures. If they are from the same family tree, how might they have gotten across continents from a common site? Present your opinions stating what you think and why.

MENTAL MIXTURES

If one of these creatures were ever captured, what could be done with it? How would scientists study the creature? Where would a safe place be to house this type of animal? Develop a "Plan for Study" that might be used to capture this elusive creature.

MOVING BEYOND

Giant Squid	Godzilla	J. Goodall
King Kong	Orangutans	Paleoanthropology
Yerkes Primate Center	Zoology	

Black Holes

A black hole is the "ghost" of a burned-out star. It has been compressed to tremendous density. Enormous gravitational forces are at work around and near a black hole. These forces prevent all light rays from escaping the space around it.

A black hole that is the same mass as Earth would be approximately the size of this black spot (•). The gravitational pull of a black hole is 100 million times that of Earth. Any matter near it is sucked in and forever trapped. If the "spot" above were a solid sphere and dropped from a height of six feet, it would probably plow into the ground to a depth of 100 feet!

There may be families of black holes in the universe billions of times more massive than the sun or perhaps "mini holes" that are microscopic in size. Some scientists have speculated that black holes might form tunnels into entirely different universes. This is surely science-fiction come to life! The vastness of space does not give up its secrets easily; it simply amazes us with each new discovery.

MUSINGS

Interesting free materials are available from the following:

Smithsonian Astrophysical Observatory
Public Information Department
60 Garden Street
Cambridge, MA 02138

MENTAL MIXTURES

What might be on the other side of black holes? Use your imagination! Brainstorm a list of possibilities to explain this.

MOVING BEYOND

Asteroids
Meteorites
Nova/Supernova

Comets
Mount Palomar Observatory

Galaxies
Neutron Stars

The Catalan Atlas

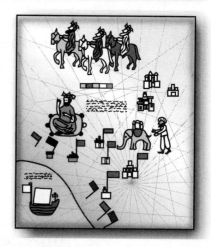

The Catalan Atlas is one of the earliest and best maps of the earth. It was created in the fourteenth century. Most remarkable were the commentaries included with the map and information regarding knowledge of the time. Among these are astronomy, astrology, and the zodiac. The seven known planets are named, and there is information on seasons and constellations. Seas, oceans, and important ports of the time are named. The spherical shape of the earth is shown. Information on tides and telling the time at night is also given. All were invaluable navigational aids for sailors voyaging to India and China. Noted places throughout the mid-eastern countries are identified and noted. The atlas is a remarkable piece of work and most incredible for that early period of time. This 65 x 300-centimeter map is one that has astonished geographers and cartographers (mapmakers) for years.

MUSINGS

1. Using a meter stick and chalk, sketch the size of the Catalan Atlas on the floor. What would this measurement be approximately in feet and inches?

2. The Majorcan Cartographic School of the fourteenth century is credited with developing the map. Majorca is an island in the Mediterranean Sea off the coast of Spain. Research this special school and summarize findings in a short paragraph.

MENTAL MIXTURES

Construct a map of your home area without referring to local maps. Include main streets in the area, roads, and other features. Can you do all this from memory? Time how long it takes to do this. How might the Catalan Atlas makers have included so much on the map when they stayed in one place?

MOVING BEYOND

Astrolabe

Cartography

Lighthouses

Magellan

Navigation

Prince Henry the Navigator

Oronteus Finaeus World Map

Portolan Maps

Wind Rose

Cheops—The Great Pyramid

Ten miles south of Cairo, Egypt, the Great Pyramid of Cheops rises 160 feet from the desert floor. This amazing example of ancient architecture covers an area as large as ten football fields, with each of the approximately 2.5 million stones weighing from two to fifteen tons.

The labor force for building the Pyramid has been estimated at 100,000 people working in shifts for 30 years to build this monumental wonder. It was so precisely built that a line drawn east to west through the Pyramid and another drawn north to south, if continued, would circle the globe and divide the earth's land masses into four equal parts. Mathematicians have also calculated that the value of pi (3.1416) was incorporated into its structure.

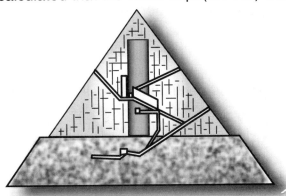

The Grand Gallery main section into the Pyramid is 150 feet in length and 25 feet high. Following the burial of King Khufu (also known as Cheops), this Grand Gallery was sealed with huge blocks that were slid down into place. The burial chamber is at the exact center of gravity. Scientists studying the Pyramid have marveled at the ability of an ancient race to cut the huge limestone and granite blocks, transport them across the desert, and set them into place. It was truly a fantastic feat of engineering for that time!

MUSINGS

The Egyptians believed in life after death. Preserving the body by mummification was developed about 2600 B.C. for this purpose. Kings were entombed surrounded by the material treasures of their lives to enjoy life in the "hereafter." Examine illustrations of tomb interiors and construct a shoebox diorama of the interior.

MENTAL MIXTURES

The Pyramid of Cheops is an example of a huge ancient structure built without the use of bulldozers, cranes, or other heavy equipment. How might this have been accomplished? Draw your ideas in a series of sketches to show "how to" build a pyramid.

MOVING BEYOND

Cartouche	Mummification	Ramses II
Sphinx	Temple of Karnak	Tutankhamen

The Coelacanth

In 1938, fishermen off the coast of South Africa pulled a strange fish out of the water. Almost five feet long, the fish had a top fin that looked normal, while the fins on its sides were thick, resembling stubby legs rather than fins. Never having seen anything like this before, the fishermen called a top *ichthyologist* (a zoologist who specializes in the study of fish) to the scene. By the time he arrived, much of the fish had rotted away in the hot African climate. Examining the head and a few bones, he was astonished to conclude that this specimen was thought to have lived in prehistoric times and disappeared from Earth many years ago during the dinosaur age. It was known as a coelacanth (see-la-canth). He claimed this was a "living fossil."

Fourteen years later, a second coelacanth was discovered near the same site. Observing that the fins again resembled legs, it was concluded that the fish probably crept as well as swam. Could this be an early relative of amphibians? In July 1998, a whole population of the coelacanth was discovered off the Indonesian coast. It is a "living laboratory" for scientists from around the world. Deep-sea diving equipment designed to study them at depths of 300 feet has enabled scientists to observe the coelacanth living in caves and diving to depths of 600 feet searching for food. Coelacanths have live births like land mammals and care for their young. This remarkable creature has provided new information and insights into the understanding of prehistoric times.

MUSINGS

1. With paired fleshy fins that move like arms or legs and an extra lobe on the tail, the coelacanth could have moved from land to water and back. With this ability, how could they have avoided detection for so long? State three ideas and a reason for each.

2. Coelacanth displays are exhibited in the Australian Museum, the French Museum of Natural History, and the Museum of Natural History in New York City. Look for these sites on the Internet and take a "tour" to find out more about this creature.

MENTAL MIXTURES

Dr. J. L. B. Smith was the noted ichthyologist called to the first discovery of the coelacanth. His book *Old Fourlegs* is an account of his findings. Write an article describing his discovery as it might have appeared in local newspapers.

MOVING BEYOND

Jacques Cousteau

Giant Squid

Ichthyology

Lungfish

Moby Dick

Oceanography

The Dead Sea Scrolls

In 1947, a goat wandered away from two Arab shepherds on the rocky coast of the Dead Sea in Israel. Four hundred feet up the side of the cliffs searching for their goat, they found an opening in one of the many small caves near the top. Throwing a stone inside to frighten the goat out of hiding, they heard a sound like the clatter of broken pottery. The shepherds crawled inside, and in the dim light, they discovered several tall covered jars. They removed the lids and found old rolls of brittle parchment covered with writing.

Archaeologists were called in to further explore the caves. Many more jars were found filled with similar parchments, dating back to 68 B.C. Tens of thousands of scroll fragments were found in 11 different caves in the same area. They were all written in Hebrew, Greek, and Aramaic. The scrolls became known as the Qumran or the Dead Sea Scrolls. By using painstaking methods to maintain the parchment, the contents were studied, and new glimpses and understandings have been gained of the past millennia. Study continues even now to learn more about the past.

MUSINGS

Make a parchment-like scroll. Crumple a sheet of paper. Wet a tea bag and wipe it all over the surface of the paper. After drying, tear uneven small pieces from around the edges. Using a thin line black marker, create a message and sign your name. Display this in the classroom.

MENTAL MIXTURES

The unusual climate of the Dead Sea area—very high evaporation with low humidity—created a favorable environment for the preservation of materials like the scrolls. Who might have written them? Why were they hidden in caves? What do you think? Write a short paragraph describing your views.

MOVING BEYOND

Artifact

Library of Alexandria

Scribe

Egyptologists

Papyrus

Fossil

Potsherds

The Drake Plate

"bee it knowne unto all men by theie presents—ivne 17, 1579—by the grace of god and in the name of herr majesty queen elizabeth of England and herr successors forever I take possession of this kingdome whose king and people freely resigne their right and title in the whole land unto her maiesties keeping now named by me an to bee knowne unto all men as nova albion. FRANCIS DRAKE."

This is an exact copy from the Drake Plate found in the 1930s on the California coast. It was believed to have been carved on the order of Sir Francis Drake, captain of the *Golden Hind,* the ship that carried him on his famous voyage around the world from 1577 to 1580. The *Golden Hind* was a mighty 102 feet in length and 20 feet in width. Drake's legendary travels and discoveries made him one of the most respected of all English sea captains of the time.

There is an account by members of Drake's crew that he left a "plate of brasse" nailed to a post somewhere in the area of Marin County, California. However, the plate found in 1937 has been proven to be a fake. It was planted in the area in 1933 as a hoax.

The real Drake Plate has never been found. Does it really exist? Drake did visit the area near San Francisco to stop and repair his ship, but no evidence of the expedition has been found.

MUSINGS

1. In the quote above, you will notice a lot of "old English" spellings. Rewrite a modern, correctly spelled and edited version of the inscription on the counterfeit Drake Plate.

2. Sir Francis Drake was known as a dashing, daring figure in England. Read about him and write a biographical summary describing his life and times.

MENTAL MIXTURES

The Drake voyage took almost three years. Recent film epics have shown how sailors of this period lived and worked aboard ship for extended periods. Pretend you are a "mate" on one of these voyages keeping a journal of experiences. Describe daily life aboard the ship, explaining how you feel about being away from home for so long. How does this compare to the journey of the Pilgrims?

MOVING BEYOND

English "Sea Dogs"	*Half Moon*	Magellan
Mayflower	Spanish Armada	Tall Ships

Amelia Earhart

Born in Atchison, Kansas, in 1890, Amelia Earhart wanted to learn how to fly. Her parents thought that this was "unladylike." It was not a pursuit for a young girl!

During World War I, Amelia was able to sign up as a military nurse and later served as a social worker. Throughout these experiences, she never lost her desire to fly and was finally able to take lessons and realize her dream. She achieved fame in 1928 when she became the first female to fly across the Atlantic Ocean. In 1932, she received financial backing to become the first female to fly across the Atlantic on a solo flight.

Continually striving for new challenges, Amelia and a copilot set off on an around-the-world trip in 1937. After completing almost two-thirds of their journey, radio contact was lost suddenly somewhere near Howland Island in the South Pacific on July 2. Air and sea searches proved futile. To this day the mystery persists—what might have happened to this famous aviatrix?

MUSINGS

1. Amelia Earhart was to maintain radio contact with the ship *Itasca* that was afloat in the Pacific Ocean. Read about how this communication was lost and write a short paragraph entitled, "Lost."

2. Using *aviation* as a key word, search the Internet and record websites for information about early aviation. Set up a list of what you think are the best sites for this topic.

3. It might be possible to have a speaker for the class if any parent is associated with an airline. Prepare questions in advance of the talk and don't forget to send a "thank you" note afterwards!

MENTAL MIXTURES

What might Amelia Earhart think if she visited an airport today? Be a reporter for the local newspaper and describe what you think her reactions and thoughts might be. Think of a catchy headline for the story.

MOVING BEYOND

Archeopteryx	Astronauts	Biplanes
Daedalus, Icarus, Pegasus	Charles Lindbergh	Wright Brothers

Easter Island

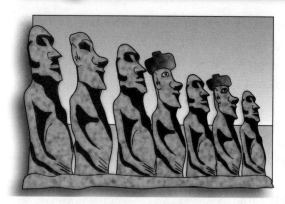

On Easter Sunday, 1722, Dutch Admiral Jacob Roggeveen and his crew accidentally discovered an uncharted island in the mid-South Pacific. When the men went ashore, they found that incredible rock structures, some 50 feet high with an average weight of 90 tons, had been strategically placed around the coast of the island. On rock platforms, each giant was the carved upper torso of a man with long ears, and some had headpieces. All were faced looking toward the sea.

One hundred years later when serious exploration began, the statues were proven to be carved from volcanic rock found inside a dormant crater on the island. Over 600 of the statues had been carved, lowered down the crater walls, moved to a specific spot, and placed in their upright positions on platforms. Many statues were found uncompleted with ancient chisels and hatchets lying nearby. Natives of the island were never found. Their disappearance is still a mystery. Only the silent guardian monoliths remain as keepers of the secret!

MUSINGS

1. Brainstorm a list of reasons to account for the carving and setting up of the statues.

2. Select one brainstormed reason as the most possible and state why this might be.

3. Examine pictures of the statues and draw a scale model. Use graph paper as a guide to help with the scale.

MENTAL MIXTURES

The ancient carvers of Easter Island might be likened to those of other ancient civilizations. Set up a chart to compare different sites where huge stone monoliths have been used in the construction of an ancient site. What tools were used, what materials were used, how were the monoliths moved, etc.? Compare possible reasons for these structures.

MOVING BEYOND

Archipelago

Polynesia

Earthquakes

Sculpture

Hawaiian Islands

Volcanoes

Ghost Towns

The quest for gold—since ancient times—has caused many men and women to abandon common sense and seek their fortunes. In this country, the discovery of gold at Sutter's Mill, California, spurred the great gold rush of the 1840s and 1850s. Within a month of the announcement of the discovery, 61 ships carrying gold seekers began the trip down the Atlantic Coast, around the tip of South America, and up the Pacific Coast to strike it rich. Gold seekers also came from all over the United States by stagecoach and covered wagons.

Whether panning for gold or working in a mine, the lure of discovery was at a fever pitch. Towns were quickly built to meet the needs of the treasure prospectors, providing stables, general stores, barber parlors, mining supplies, and a "hot" shower. The most important place was the assayer's office where new gold finds could be tested and appraised. Sadly, the search proved futile for many. Running out of money and unable to make any claims, they left for home. The towns soon became deserted—sad witnesses to the prospectors' lack of luck. All that survives today are the remnants of a teeming and boisterous era in history. Some claim that sorrowful sounds still echo through the remnants of "what might have been."

MUSINGS

1. Try to imagine what a trip to California might have been like in the days of the gold rush. Do some reading about the period. Set up a journal and describe the trip, hardships along the way, and your feelings about finding gold. Describe the closest "town."

2. Many events in history have been commemorated with the creation of special postage stamps. Design a stamp for the gold rush. Think of a suitable picture and colors for the stamp. Use art paper to make an enlarged drawing of it. (It might be helpful to note some of the designs used on stamps today.)

MENTAL MIXTURES

The gold rush was one of the major ways in which the west was settled. As mines developed throughout these areas, more people arrived. Many made land claims and stayed. Some came by wagon trains to farm and raise cattle. Merchants also came to supply the miners and other settlers. On an outline map of the United States, show some of the major routes used by settlers on their way west.

MOVING BEYOND

William F. Cody	Wyatt Earp	Gold Bullion
Gold Mining	Annie Oakley	Western Expansion

The Great Wall of China

What may be the most ambitious construction project of all time winds 2,150 miles from the gulf of the Yellow Sea in the east to China's western border with Mongolia. Built of bricks on a granite foundation, the wall rises 40 feet in height with a walkway on top of it that is 15 feet wide. Sentry towers were placed 200 yards apart. In each tower a sentry was posted, sometimes for the duration of his life.

Begun about 403 B.C. by Emperor Shih Huang, over two million men were used in the construction process over a period of 20 years. Thousands of laborers perished on the job and were buried within the wall as construction continued, making it the world's largest necropolis (cemetery) as well as the longest fortification.

The Great Wall is so huge that is it is one of the only man-made structures seen by astronauts on NASA flights and photographed by orbiting satellites. If stretched out, the wall would cover a distance equal to the length of the United States and Canadian border!

MUSINGS

1. The Great Wall was probably a boundary marker and fortification against raids from Tatar enemies. Find pictures of this structure and sketch a section showing a sentry tower.

2. Using a dictionary, define these fortification terms: parapet, sallyport, magazine, bastion, moat, and turret.

MENTAL MIXTURES

Man has always been concerned with safety, security, and protection. Investigate safety measures at school by interviewing a safety officer (if there is one) or a person in administration. What measures are the most important? Which are standards for all schools? Should any be added?

MOVING BEYOND

The Alamo   Berlin Wall   Bimini Wall
Forts: Caroline, McHenry, Pulaski, Sumter   Hadrian's Wall
Masada   Medieval Castles

The Hindenburg

THE CHICAGO DAILY NEWS

HINDENBURG EXPLODES, BURNS. FEAR 90 KILLED

Giant Zeppelin Was Landing at Lakehurst Base

Hindenburg Bursts Into Flames After Explosion

The *Hindenburg* was a zeppelin, a lighter-than-air rigid airship. The first zeppelin was invented by Count Ferdinand von Zeppelin, and it was launched in 1900. It was the first step in establishing a new means of transportation. By 1914, over 35,000 passengers had been carried without a single accident on these wondrous hydrogen gas airships. The *Hindenburg* was the largest zeppelin ever built. It could travel at a good speed and did not need refueling for almost 10,000 miles.

In May 1937, the *Hindenburg* left Frankfurt, Germany, heading across the Atlantic Ocean to Lakehurst, New Jersey. The flight was going well until it was ready to dock. Suddenly, a fire started, and in 34 seconds, the entire ship was destroyed in a massive fire. How did this happen? Was it an act of sabotage? A fuel leak? The questions still persist.

MUSINGS

1. One of the most famous radio news broadcasts was made by a reporter at the scene of the disaster in Lakehurst. He spoke hysterically while describing the terrible event and then broke into tears. Research this historical broadcast. Describe your reactions.

2. Construct a time line of air transportation development from 1900 to the present. Make the sections 15 years apart. Add illustrations of some of the significant events.

MENTAL MIXTURES

Airships are still used today for traffic control, mail delivery, advertising, and broadcasting. What might be an interesting new use for these giants of the air? Draw your idea of an interesting use and label the important features it would need.

MOVING BEYOND

Blimps and Dirigibles	Early Aviation	Gliders
Graf Zeppelin	Hot Air Ballooning	Charles Lindbergh

The Hope Diamond

This beautiful gem is one of the most perfectly cut, deep-blue diamonds in the world. Weighing 44 carats, the Hope Diamond has a history of doom that reaches back to the 1600s when Jean Tavernier brought it to Paris. Rumors about the diamond's history hint that Tavernier had stolen it from a sacred idol in India, and that, as a result, it was cursed. King Louis XIV paid a fortune for it, not caring about any curse it might have. Years later, Tavernier lost the money and died penniless. Louis' descendant Louis XVI gave it to his wife, Marie Antoinette. Both were beheaded during the French Revolution, and the diamond was stolen. It showed up again in 1830 when Henry Hope bought it and then later sold it in 1901.

One by one, new owners came to bad ends, until the diamond was finally donated to the Smithsonian Institute in Washington, D.C., where it is usually exhibited. Were these misfortunes coincidences? We might never know. However, the beauty of the Hope Diamond remains for all to see.

MUSINGS

1. Diamonds are mined in specific locations around the world. Find out where some of the major mining areas are, and investigate how diamonds are mined. Show the steps in pictorial sequence.

2. Design and make a poster advertisement for the Hope Diamond that the Smithsonian Institute might use to encourage visitors to view the exhibit.

MENTAL MIXTURES

The Hermitage is a world-famous museum in St. Petersburg, Russia. It contains the world's largest collection of art and jewelry dating back over two centuries to the reign of Catherine the Great. Choose any three famous museums and gather information about their locations, size, and special exhibits. Some examples from which to choose are the Prado, Louvre, British Museum, Smithsonian, Guggenheim, and the National Gallery of Art.

MOVING BEYOND

Amber	British Crown Jewels	Gemology
Mohs Scale	Star of India	Turquoise

Houdini

Harry Houdini was a daring magician at the turn of the twentieth century. He was known as the "Great Escape Artist." Audiences were dazzled and puzzled by his escapes from handcuffs, locks, sealed boxes, and any other device set for him.

Always reading, researching, and practicing his craft, Houdini was always searching for unusual methods to use in his act. He was the most innovative performer of his time. He developed a method to contract and expand his body muscles at will and hold them that way for several minutes. When shackled and placed underwater, he could fill his lungs with air and hold it for a period of time in order to accomplish the many water submersion feats he performed.

All of Houdini's methods were based on his knowledge of science and scientific calculations to figure out the exact amount of air his lungs could hold, the maximum time he could hold his breath, and the measurements of his muscles when expanded and relaxed. He was so precise and so careful that his accidental death from an injury suffered during one of his stunts was unbelievable to his fans all over the world. He greatly influenced and advanced the science of performing magic for generations.

MUSINGS

1. How did Houdini die? Read about this unusual event and write a brief report explaining what happened.

2. In one escape, Houdini was cuffed and manacled, locked in a trunk, and turned upside down in a tank of water on stage. Create a newspaper story about this event. Think up a catchy headline!

MENTAL MIXTURES

After a performance career of more than 25 years, Houdini died at the age of 53. His wife Bess donated his huge personal library of 5,200 books to the Library of Congress in Washington, D.C. Look up the meaning of *epitaph* and then write a fitting one for this great magician.

MOVING BEYOND

Harry Blackstone

Magic Tricks

David Copperfield

Merlin the Magician

Library of Congress

Optical Illusions

King Arthur

"I'm not a king of the country, I'm a king of the people."—*Arthur*

"Men who pray, men who fight, and men who work, this was the model for a well-run kingdom."—*King Alfred (871–899)*

Arthur of Pendragon, King Arthur, Ruler of Camelot, and founder of the Knights of the Round Table were all names given to the legendary hero, Arthur. Symbolic of the best qualities in man, Arthurian legends have been told and passed down through the generations for 1,500 years. He is a cherished British tradition, rooted in early fifth-century history. His reputation as a wise ruler, being tutored by Merlin, pulling the sword Excalibur from a stone, and his fame as a brave warrior who led his troops to defeat invading Saxon enemies endear him to the hearts of all.

According to a mixture of fact and legend, Arthur was a real hero and king, but the mystery remains, and proof is difficult to obtain. Did Arthur really exist? Was there a Camelot? During the presidency of John F. Kennedy, many people likened his term in office to that of King Arthur's because it was said that he followed the same ideals of the legends. During Kennedy's presidency, Washington, D.C., was called the "new Camelot."

MUSINGS

1. Set up an "Arthurian" glossary. Explain each of the following and add illustrations: Merlin, Guinevere, Camelot, Excalibur, Sir Lancelot, the Knights of the Round Table, knighthood, the Holy Grail, and heraldry. Share your findings with classmates.

2. Knights carried shields decorated with symbols related to their families. Create a shield for your family. Think of symbols that could represent family experiences. Enlarge the shield on art paper and display it in the classroom.

3. Read about medieval times: *Beowulf's Fight With Grendel* by Mabie, *Roland and His Horn* by Cox, and *How St. George Fought the Dragon* by Lansing.

MENTAL MIXTURES

Arthur was a hero of his time. What makes a hero? Who are some heroes of today? List adjectives suitable to describe heroes. Make a "Favorite Heroes" list of five people you consider heroes. Explain why each was chosen.

MOVING BEYOND

Alexander the Great	Charlemagne	Feudal System
Heraldry	Sir Thomas Malory	Tournaments/Jousting

Lighthouse Mystery

The first lighthouse was built in Egypt in 280 B.C., starting a long tradition as guides and beacons of safety for those at sea. Early light-keepers spent lonely lives as they provided this needed maritime service. The lighthouses of today have electric "eyes" that activate a light beam as evening approaches and automatic sensors that turn foghorns on when moisture in the air signals the coming of fog. However, the "human touch" is still needed.

An unusual story involves the Saint Simons Island, Georgia, lighthouse. The lighthouse was destroyed and rebuilt several times after a Spanish invasion and the Civil War. The lighthouse keeper was killed in 1880. Events surrounding his death are not clear. His lonely life ended in a mystery. The tread of footsteps heard on the spiral staircase of the tower are said to be his as he walks up to the tower each night to check the beacon. Keepers throughout the years have retold this traditionally popular story, especially around the Halloween season! Viewing the area on a cold night can provide some "chills." Currently, the keeper's cottage is opened to the public as a museum.

MUSINGS

1. Prepare a want ad for a lighthouse keeper. List the questions to be asked during an interview with someone applying for the job. What special traits would be necessary for the keeper's position?

2. Whalers searched for the stream of vapor blown toward the sky as a sign that a whale was nearby. "There she blows!" was the signal to lower small whaleboats into the sea and get ready to use harpoons. Whalers formed a large part of the sea traffic in the mid-1800s. *Moby Dick* is a classic story about this period. Use it as a reading project and prepare an oral report for the class as if you were Captain Ahab.

MENTAL MIXTURES

Find and examine pictures of lighthouses and their special features. Construct a lighthouse diorama. On another sheet of paper, make a sketch of what the interior might look like.

MOVING BEYOND

Clipper Ships	Fire Island	Lime Rock
Minot's Ledge	Pharos of Alexandria	Scrimshaw
Whaling Ships		

Lincoln, Kennedy

One of the most curious ironies of history involves the similarities that existed between the lives of Presidents Abraham Lincoln and John F. Kennedy. Read and be amazed …

1. Both were assassinated on a Friday in the presence of their wives.

2. Their successors were both named Johnson: Andrew Johnson and Lyndon Baines Johnson.

3. John Wilkes Booth, Lincoln's assassin, was born in 1839. Lee Harvey Oswald, Kennedy's assassin, was born in 1939.

4. Kennedy's personal secretary's last name was Lincoln. Lincoln's secretary's last name was Kennedy.

5. Lincoln and Kennedy are each seven-letter names.

6. The names John Wilkes Booth and Lee Harvey Oswald each contain 15 letters.

7. Lincoln was elected president in 1860, Kennedy in 1960.

8. Both presidents were concerned with civil rights.

MUSINGS

1. There are many qualities of leadership. Which should a president have? Brainstorm a list of these qualities and explain why each is important.

2. There are many other similarities regarding Lincoln and Kennedy. Investigate to find out what these are. Set up a chart to compare your findings with your classmates'.

MENTAL MIXTURES

Many official and unofficial qualifications have to be met in order to run for President of the United States. Find out what these are and include them in a "presidential want ad."

MOVING BEYOND

Electoral College	Ford's Theatre	Mount Rushmore
Oath of Office	Presidential Libraries	The White House

The Loch Ness Creature

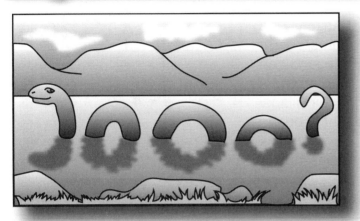

For hundreds of years, stories have been told about a creature living in Scotland's Loch Ness. Loch Ness is a lake (loch) 22 miles long and two miles wide that was formed by the melting of Ice Age glaciers about 10,000 years ago.

About A.D. 565, stories of a creature were told by Scotsmen who lived near the loch. They nicknamed the creature "Nessie" and described it as 50 feet in length with a seal-like body and long neck. The first known photograph was taken by a vacationing London doctor in 1933 showing a huge shadowy form swimming in the murky water. It is probably the most famous photograph ever taken. Following this, word of the creature spread and took on a new image. It could be real!

Numerous scientific teams from around the world have gone to the loch to conduct investigations through the years. In recent times, using the latest technological equipment available, sonar showed traces of large objects moving rapidly through the water. Prehistoric stone formations were also discovered on the bottom of the loch and in nearby underwater caves.

Theories abound about "Nessie's" existence. The creature might be a long-necked seal, a long-tailed salamander-like amphibian, a giant eel, or a prehistoric creature that somehow became trapped in the loch as the Ice Age glaciers receded. As yet, there are no definite answers.

MUSINGS

1. Draw a map of Scotland and locate Loch Ness. Include geographic borders of the country and water features that are near the loch.

2. "Nessie" has been described as a large dinosaur, fish, eel, and newt. Which do you agree with? Sketch your idea and explain why you agree with this particular theory.

3. An expedition is preparing to investigate the loch. Make an equipment list of necessary items. Include the types of scientists that should be included on the team.

MENTAL MIXTURES

Earlier in this book is the puzzle of the coelacanth. How do theories about this creature compare with "Nessie"? Construct a chart showing similarities and differences. Are there other creatures that might have survived from prehistoric times?

MOVING BEYOND

Amphibians	Blue Whale	Dinosaurs
Giant Squid	Great White Shark	Ice Age

The Lost Dutchman Mine

Deep in the Superstition Mountains of Arizona, the quest for a gold mine has lured thousands of prospectors through the years. The Lost Dutchman Mine legend can be traced back to the early 1800s when three brothers discovered the mine and brought gold back to their village. When the greedy villagers saw the gold, they began searching the mountain areas for the gold. The mountains were sacred to the Apache tribe. For trespassing in the mountains, the Apaches ambushed and killed the searchers. Only one of the three brothers, Don Miguel Peralta, managed to escape. He was saved from the Apaches by Jacob Walzer, a Dutchman who lived in the area. To thank him, Peralta told Walzer the location of the mine. Walzer supposedly found it, but the secret disappeared with him when he was also killed.

The mine was forgotten until 1914, when $200,000 in gold ore was found near the village. Did it come from the mine? This is the question that continues to intrigue treasure hunters. There are no known mines in the area, and no minerals of any kind have ever been found in the wilderness of the Superstition Mountains.

MUSINGS

1. Fact versus fiction. Myth versus legend. These are terms used in many of these mysteries. Use a dictionary and write the meaning for each term.

2. Create a map showing your idea of the location of the Lost Dutchman Mine. Find the Superstition Mountains and other land features on a real map before you design the treasure map.

MENTAL MIXTURES

Gold is a global standard used to assess the value of money. What money do we use? Who appears on the $5, $10, $20, $50, and $100 bills? Do classmates know? Find out, and then conduct a survey of classmates. How many know about money? Report your findings when the survey is completed.

MOVING BEYOND

Great Depression   J.P. Morgan   Rockefeller Family
U.S. Mint in Denver   U.S. Treasury   Vanderbilt Family

Machu Picchu

Hiram Bingham, an American explorer, discovered the remains of the ancient city of Machu Picchu in 1911. Situated 2,000 feet above sea level in the Andes Mountains near Cuzco, Peru, Machu Picchu stands as a lasting testimony to the work of one of the greatest groups of ancient stonemasons and builders, the Incas.

Archaeologists exploring the region over the years have identified such structures at Machu Picchu as private dwellings, stairways, terraces, irrigation systems, stone basins, and baths. The finest example of a sundial or "intihuctana" can be seen at this location. It was used as an astronomical calculator for the ritual worship of the sun. All the cut stones are so expertly and closely fitted that a sheet of paper can barely slide between them. Earthquakes in the area through the years have barely affected Machu Picchu.

The great structures of Machu Picchu are examples of tremendous engineering insight and present an awe-inspiring sight to all who view them.

MUSINGS

1. Using a sheet of art paper, set up an Incan scrapbook. Include pictures of structures, religious and cultural beliefs, and hunting and food-gathering methods. Their style of dress and pottery are other areas to examine.

2. Write for free information from: The Center for Archaeological Research, University of Texas, San Antonio, Texas, 78285. Be specific in the request and have your teacher or parent sign the letter as well. Some of the material and pictures can be used in the scrapbook.

3. To find information and illustrations of over 750 structures, visit this web address: www. greatbuildings.com.

MENTAL MIXTURES

Write a report using the title "Centuries of Great Builders." Include what you have learned about huge structures around the world. How do they compare? Which ancient group of builders had the most skill? What was the purpose of the structures? If you could travel to one of them, which would it be? Why?

MOVING BEYOND

Anthropology	Archaeology	City of Ur, Ancient Sumeria
Luxor	Teotihuacán, Pyramid of the Sun	Valley of the Kings

The Mary Celeste

On December 4, 1872, the ship *Dei Gratia* was 20 days from New York in the North Atlantic. On board were Captain David Morehouse and a crew of seven. A ship was sighted that seemed to be moving erratically. Morehouse tried to hail the ship through his speaking trumpet, but received no response.

The first mate and several men were sent in a small boat to investigate.

Boarding the ship, the *Mary Celeste,* they found that it was deserted. The captain's clothing and that of a woman and child, an assortment of toys, money, jewelry, and furniture was found. Laundry was hanging on a line, the living quarters of the crew contained pipes and tobacco, and there were coins on the table. Everything appeared as if the occupants had just stepped outside for a few moments. Plenty of food and water were available in the clean ship's galley, and all the equipment was neatly stored. One lifeboat was gone, as well as all the ship's papers and navigational instruments. No mention of any problem was written in the captain's log. There was no evidence of fire, collision, or struggle.

The ship was eventually towed to Gibraltar, refurbished, and sailed again with a new crew and captain. The original crew, captain, and family were never heard from again. In the court of inquiry that followed, no logical explanation could be determined as to why the *Mary Celeste* had been abandoned. For the first time in the court's history, a definite conclusion could not be found.

MUSINGS

1. For interesting information about the *Mary Celeste*, consult the Dictionary of Disasters at Sea. You can also write to: The U.S. Maritime Agency, Washington, D.C., 20003 for free information.

2. Write an entry for the ship's log that the captain might have made regarding circumstances that caused the sudden disappearances.

MENTAL MIXTURES

None of the important navigational tools were aboard the ship. Find out about the type of instruments used aboard ships during this time period, such as chronometer, sextant, and compass. Formulate a theory about the reason(s) for the disappearance of the ship.

MOVING BEYOND

Andrea Doria	HMS *Bounty*	SS *Lusitania*
Maritime Law	SS *Titanic*	Tall Ships

The Mayas

The Mayas were a Central American jungle tribe whose culture was more sophisticated than any other in ancient South America. Using primitive tools, they constructed great cities, created a language, charted the stars, and designed beautiful sculptures. With startling accuracy and knowledge of astronomy, they could follow the movements of the stars and predict lunar eclipses. Their writing method was composed of picture symbols, and their mathematics enabled them to calculate in the hundreds of millions. They were skilled surgeons who could perform brain surgery.

At its peak, the Mayan kingdom extended 550 miles north to south and 350 miles east to west in Mexico, Guatemala, and Belize. Many Mayan cities had populations of over 50,000. A distinctive class system of hereditary nobles, priests, and rulers was in place. From A.D. 300 to 900, they built magnificent cities with pyramids 17 stories high and palaces with more than 100 rooms.

The Mayan civilization began to decline at the beginning of the tenth century. About two million of their descendants survive today on 150,000 square miles of the Yucatán Peninsula. Hundreds of thousands still speak variations of the ancient dialects and practice the beliefs and rituals of that time.

MUSINGS

1. Construct the Mayan number system using any of the following materials: sticks and small stones, straws and buttons or macaroni, or any materials that could substitute for the system. Mount them on art paper and label each number.

1 = •	2 = ••	3 = •••	4 = ••••	5 = ____
6 = •/____	7 = ••/____	8 = •••/____	9 = ••••/____	10 = ____/____

What would the symbol be for 25? 16? 30?

2. Write for free information to the: Mexican Information Office, Dept. 0-08 Mexico House, 9445 Wilshire Blvd., Beverly Hills, CA 90212. Be sure to use the correct letter format!

MENTAL MIXTURES

The loss of the Mayan civilization is the loss of a culture we might have learned a great deal about. If our culture were explored 1,000 years from now, what items would best represent our lives? List eight to ten things you think would be important for a future understanding of our way of life. State a reason for each item.

MOVING BEYOND

Chichén Itzá	Cozumel	Mayan Calendar	Palenque
Pyramid of the Sun	Tulum	Uxmal	

The Mona Lisa

The *Mona Lisa,* also known as *La Gioconda*, or the lady with the mystical smile, is one of Leonardo da Vinci's most famous masterpieces. What accounted for her expression? What did she represent? There have always been many unanswered questions about this mysterious lady.

Over one million people a year visit this portrait, displayed in the Louvre museum in Paris, France. The painting was done in 1503. Da Vinci was the first artist of his time to create the human image as a real form. Before his time, portraits were stylized and idealized, following the popular style of the period. When the Mona Lisa was seen for the first time, viewers felt that they were in the presence of a living being. They saw a woman fashionably dressed with a strange smile on her face, seated in front of a delicate background landscape, her hands gently folded.

Leonardo da Vinci started a new method of painting for his era and changed the course of art from then on. In recent times, the *Mona Lisa* again gained wide attention as it was sent on loan for a world tour of museums. Globally, people could have the experience of viewing this great masterpiece.

MUSINGS

1. Find a picture of the *Mona Lisa* painting and stand it up so you can view it at eye level. Move slowly back and forth in front of it, not moving your eyes from her eyes. What happens? Describe your experience to the class.

2. It is said that da Vinci was born 400 years ahead of his time. A man of great vision and genius, da Vinci was also a sculptor, inventor, and biologist. He wrote hundreds of notebooks about his findings, including sketches, and all the words were written backwards! Prepare a biographical summary of this astounding man.

MENTAL MIXTURES

"No man in recorded history exemplifies the inventive capacity of mankind more than the fifteenth-century genius, Leonardo da Vinci. He investigated virtually every field of science. He recorded practical solutions to specific problems and explored such future possibilities as a flying machine, automobiles, and automatons."—IBM Corporation. Find out about some of da Vinci's inventions. List five that you think are the most unusual for his time. Explain why you chose each one.

MOVING BEYOND

Botticelli	British Museum	Guggenheim Museum
Michelangelo	The Prado	Raphael

30

The Money Pit

In 1795 as three youths explored Oak Island, one of the many islands in Mahone Bay off the Nova Scotia coast, they discovered a ship's tackle block hanging from the lower limb of a tree. Upon closer inspection, they saw a depression under the tree and started digging. Tales of pirate treasure lured them to investigate further.

Digging in the suspicious area, they found themselves enclosed in a thirteen-foot-wide shaft on a stone layer at a depth of 10 feet. As they continued to dig, an oak log platform was seen. They dragged the logs away and kept digging to a depth of 30 feet. Each separate layer they found was preceded by similar log platforms. Exhausted, they finally stopped digging and went home.

Word soon got out, and other groups attempted to dig throughout the years. At first, oak platforms were discovered every 10 feet. Finally, at a depth of 90 feet, a large horizontal stone with strange markings was found. These markings have never been deciphered. An elaborate tunnel system was also discovered that continuously flooded into the main shaft to heights of 65 feet, depending on the rise and fall of the tides.

In 1895, a group of adventurers drilled down to 151 feet and hit a two-inch-thick cemented area. Even electric pumps proved futile for later explorers. To this day, no one has yet been able to dig any deeper or find treasure, if any exists. Who built this strange pit? What was hidden, if anything?

MUSINGS

1. Draw a map of Oak Island showing the location of the Money Pit site.

2. Construct a shoebox diorama of the Money Pit. Use the box in a vertical position showing the different layers. Set up a scale so distances can be approximated.

MENTAL MIXTURES

What do you do with your "treasured" items? List five of those most valued and the reason each is important.

MOVING BEYOND

| British "Sea Dogs" | Lighthouses | Lost Dutchman Mine | Pirates |
| Scrimshaw | Spanish Armada | Spanish Galleons | |

Read a classic sea adventure such as: *Moby Dick, Treasure Island, Mutiny on the Bounty,* or *Rime of the Ancient Mariner.*

Mystery Skulls

During the 1930s near a small village southwest of Chihuahua, Mexico, an astounding discovery was made. At the rear of an old mine tunnel, the remains of two mysterious humans were found. One was a complete skeleton, the other a small malformed skeleton. As scientists examined the remains, they concluded that the skulls seemed to be formed from quartz, the same type used today in computers.

According to the legends of ancient Native American shamans, there are thirteen life-sized crystal skulls. Each contains information for humankind about the future. Quartz is almost entirely formed from silicon dioxide and is found in almost every kind of rock. No one has yet been able to establish a date or place from which the skulls originated. Others have been found in Central America and Peru. The skulls remain mysterious artifacts.

MUSINGS

1. Find out about shamans, medicine men, chieftains, and kachinas. Set up a chart to compare Native American beliefs regarding these personages and the tribal roles of each.

2. Amber is a resin often containing fossil remains of long ago. Read about how this is formed and write a brief report. Add illustrations showing the kinds of fossils it holds. Compare the qualities of amber to that of quartz.

MENTAL MIXTURES

Could the skulls be artifacts or remnants from some ancient culture? Prepare a three-minute talk to present your opinion and explain why you think this.

MOVING BEYOND

Anthropology

Crystals

Fossils

Lascaux Caves

Native American Cultures

Osteology

Skeletal System

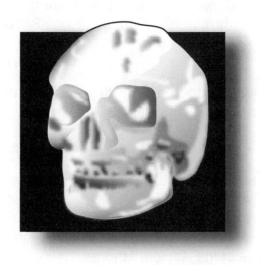

Mystery Spot

One of the strangest places in the country is located in Santa Cruz, California. Discovered in 1940, the area defies the known properties of gravity, perspective, height, and direction. Walking through this strange environment, it is difficult to keep a sense of balance or to know which way is up!

In an area about 150 feet in diameter, when walking southwest, a person can lean forward almost to a 45-degree angle and not fall. It is like being pulled forward by a heavy weight. All of the trees lean toward the center, and the sounds of insects and birds are absent. Walking along a horizontal slab of concrete, the height seems to change from one side to the other even though the ground is level. A small cabin was built over the exact center of the site. Here the pulling effect is the strongest, and you can walk halfway up the interior walls and not fall.

Scientists have investigated this unusual place, and their findings suggest the possibility of a magnetic force deep inside the earth. But how did it get there? What is it?

MUSINGS

1. Using a map of California, locate Santa Cruz. Sketch a map of the site showing bordering geographical features. Be sure to label all parts of the map and include a scale.

2. There are other places similar to this in other parts of the world. Search the Internet and set up a list of these sites and their locations. Use "magnetic spots" as a key word.

MENTAL MIXTURES

What if this "force" could be harnessed and used for other purposes? What could be invented? What would it do? Create an invention that could use this force. Label the special features it has and explain how they might work.

MOVING BEYOND

Albert Einstein	Gravity	Magnetism
Sir Isaac Newton	Spook Hill, Florida	

Nazca Lines

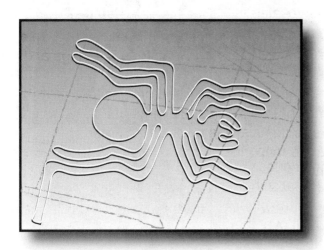

In 1927, a pilot flying over a strip of desert in Nazca, Peru, saw an incredible sight. Patterns shaped like humans and animals were etched into the earth. A fox, lizard, spider, monkey, whale, and vulture could be plainly seen. Other lines formed triangles, rectangles, and other shapes. These amazing outlines, some hundreds of feet long, are scratched into the hard surface and are about 1,500 years old.

Scientists have determined that the lines were probably made by the Nazca Indians, inhabitants of the area some 1,000 to 2,500 years ago. Seen from an airplane, the lines are a spectacular sight. At ground level, they appear as nothing more than twisted footpaths that seem to extend in different directions.

Maria Reiche, a noted mathematician, has been studying the lines for over 40 years. She has concluded that the Nazca, or "Andes" Lines, could have taken many years to carve into the earth. They might have been an ancient observatory to track certain stars or seasons. Only the ancients know what they symbolize!

MUSINGS

1. Set up a "Nazca Notes" scrapbook. Find pictures of the huge creatures carved into the earth and sketch them for the opening pages.

2. Maria Reiche has devoted much of her life to investigating the Nazca Lines. Read about her life and experiences and write a short biographical sketch. Add this to the scrapbook.

3. What geographical features border Peru? Identify these on a map and create a map of the area on another page of the scrapbook.

MENTAL MIXTURES

There are so many things in this world we still do not know about! Structures created by many ancient peoples exist globally. Many of these could have been used to determine seasons, as giant observatories, or as an early type of calendar. What do you think? Which seems the most possible? Why? Write what you think. Add your theories to the list too!

MOVING BEYOND

| American Sign Language | Cuneiform | Hieroglyphics |
| Morse Code | Papyrus | Pictographs |

The Piri Reis Map

In 1929, during a renovation of the Imperial Palace in Istanbul (what was once Constantinople), a group of historians found a map painted on gazelle skin. Dated 1513 and drawn by Piri Reis, this remarkable map showed accurate latitude and longitude markings and amazing details for that time.

Many islands along the southern coast of Antarctica were drawn, and precise locations of the South American and African coastlines were shown. This was just 21 years after Columbus sailed through the Caribbean and 300 years before Antarctica was even discovered!

As geologists and cartographers examined the map closely over the years, they have found that the accuracy of the earth's circumference shown was within 50 miles of its actual measurement. This was a remarkable feat for Piri Reis. How did he do it? Actually, Piri Reis admitted to using even older maps as sources for his map. From where did these older maps come? How could these ancient mapmakers have known so much about the world?

MUSINGS

1. Piri Reis was a famous Turkish admiral of the sixteenth century. Read about his life and times and prepare a brief biographical report.

2. Marine chronometers were time-measuring instruments that were the first instruments used to accurately calculate longitude. They were developed in England in 1771. Construct a labeled diagram of this early instrument.

MENTAL MIXTURES

By studying the moon through giant telescopes, many features and locations were named and drawn. The Sea of Tranquility is one of the major locations known. Study a map of the moon and make a list of identifiable features. Someday, man will be able to travel there for a vacation! Technology is already in the planning stage to accomplish this. Would you like to be a moon vacationer sometime in the near future?

MOVING BEYOND
Atlantic Ridge

Dulcert's Portolano

Map Projections

Marianas Trench

Steppes

Zeno's Chart

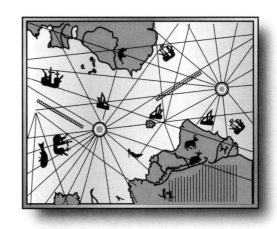

35

The Rhind Papyrus

The Rhind Papyrus is an Egyptian mathematical scroll. It measures 19 feet in length and two feet in width. It is named for the man who purchased it in Egypt in 1858, Alexander Henry Rhind. Originally discovered in Thebes, it is evidence that the Egyptians knew addition, subtraction, multiplication, and division!

Made by Ahames, an Egyptian scribe in 1650 B.C. during the fifteenth dynasty, it is one of the oldest mathematical documents known today. Numerical tables including 84 problems and their solutions are shown. Those who needed to use the mathematical computations were probably priests and priestesses who were in charge of workers, surveyors, masons, and engineers involved in building the pyramids.

The Rhind Papyrus can be seen in the British Museum in London, England. Scientists examining the past gain clearer insights into the mathematics used today. It is a more comprehensive way to enhance our current knowledge and appreciate the great accomplishments that were part of early cultures. How the systems were developed is not known, but the Rhind Papyrus is a testament to ancient computation. It is an amazing document!

MUSINGS

1. The Rhind Papyrus is one of the most famous papyri. Others include the Reisner, Berlin, Moscow, and Kakun. Select one of these for a brief report. Compare how the one you selected is alike and how it is different from the Rhind Papyrus.

2. Ancient events and items are dated B.C., A.D., and B.C.E. Find the meaning of each.

3. The early Egyptians and Greeks provided the basis for many types of mathematics including geometry. Pythagoras, Euclid, Thales of Miletus, and Archimedes are among the most famous mathematicians. Construct a chart and research to find out when they lived and the major contributions of each.

MENTAL MIXTURES

All structures are based on mathematical computation and geometry. Design a poster showing geometric shapes that are used by architects.

MOVING BEYOND

Alabaster	Ancient Thebes	Avagadro's Number
The "Golden Section"	Perimeter and Area	Symmetry

Roanoke Island—The Lost Colony

In 1587, Sir Walter Raleigh's third Virginia colony was established on Roanoke Island on the coast of what is now North Carolina. Three years after the colony was settled and thriving, a relief ship arrived from England carrying needed tools, supplies, and other provisions. After going ashore, crew members discovered, to their surprise, a deserted colony. The colonists were gone without a trace, and nothing was found to give reasons for their disappearance. The fate of 89 men, 17 women, and 11 children is still a mystery. One of the children was named Virginia Dare. She was the first child of English parents born in the "New World," America.

As the captain and his crew searched for days, they found that the fort had been dismantled, and a wood post had the strange word "Croatoan" carved on it. Croatoan was an island south of Roanoke inhabited by the friendly Hatteras Indians. No documented attempt was made by the relief expedition to find the colonists.

In the eighteenth century, settlers near the Lumber River in North Carolina were surprised to find a tribe of fair-haired, blue-eyed Indians. What could this mean? There have been no verifiable claims to date.

MUSINGS

1. Did the Indians turn against the colonists? Did a harsh winter and lack of food force survivors to go with the Indians for protection against starvation and sickness? Why were no bodies or graves found? Did the captain and his crew investigate thoroughly enough? Write a diary page as if you were one of the colonists who disappeared. Describe what might have caused your disappearance.

2. Mysterious disappearances of whole groups of people abound throughout recorded history, such as the Mayas and Incas. Write a newspaper article presenting details about how this might have happened.

3. What could "Croatoan" have meant? List three possibilities.

MENTAL MIXTURES

Between 1584 and 1587, Sir Walter Raleigh made three Roanoke voyages. The third was aboard the *Elizabeth II*. The ship was 69 feet in length and 17 feet wide. Research vessels of this period and prepare a cutaway diagram showing a typical ship of the time. Identify and label major sections.

MOVING BEYOND

English Explorations	English "Sea Dogs"	Henry Hudson
Jamestown Settlement	Pilgrims	Plymouth Colony

Robin Hood

Robin Hood was a folk hero of the British people, but did he really exist? No one knows for sure. His name first appears in the poems of Piers the Plowman in the fourteenth century, and stories about him have been handed down through the generations. Children learn about his fierce loyalty to King Richard, his activities in Sherwood Forest, his band of Merry Men, and his love for Maid Marian. Though Robin Hood was a highwayman, he "robbed from the rich and generously gave it to the poor." He delivered punishment to those who were greedy, corrupt, and took advantage of the downtrodden. He fought the Sheriff of Nottingham for the rights of the people. He was their hero during a time when the peasants needed a champion. Eventually, the Peasants' Revolt of 1381 evolved and is noted by historians as one of the events that marked the end of the Middle Ages. Was Robin Hood involved in the revolt? What was his role later in life? Many would like to know!

MUSINGS

1. Robin Hood's robbing from the rich and giving to the poor is not an acceptable behavior today. His actions would now be considered crimes. Prepare a paragraph explaining the consequences of this behavior today. What might happen?

2. There are many stories about the Merry Men who used Sherwood Forest as their camp and operations center. Friar Tuck, Little John, Will Scarlett, and Alan-A-Dale were nicknames given to them about the way they met and joined Robin Hood. Many of the tales are entertaining to read. Select one to read about and prepare a "Merry Men" report.

MENTAL MIXTURES

Many charitable agencies exist to provide services needed by people today. Kiwanis, church and synagogue groups, Optimists, the Salvation Army, and the Red Cross are just a few. What is available in your community? Search the telephone book's Yellow Pages and set up a list of agencies, how to contact them, and the specific services they provide. It may be possible to join as a volunteer.

MOVING BEYOND

Archery	Fiefdom	Forests of England
Middle Ages	Richard the Lion Heart	Social Services

The Rosetta Stone

When the armies of Napoleon invaded Egypt in the 1790s, one of his soldiers unearthed a large flat stone that was the size of a tabletop. It was covered with strange writing and was later named the Rosetta Stone because it was found near the town of Raschid (Rosetta) near the delta of the Nile River.

A slab of black basalt 3'4″ long, 2'4$\frac{1}{2}$″ wide, and 11″ thick, the Stone was covered with writing in three languages: hieroglyphics, demotic or pictographs, and Greek. They represented a single text that was a decree of praise for King Ptolemy from the priests of Memphis about 196 B.C. It took years to decipher the three languages, but archaeologists and Egyptologists finally unlocked much of the unknown meanings of the ancient Egyptian writings. An entire list of the Egyptian alphabet was collected.

Now in the British Museum in London, England, much of the translation is credited to British physicist Thomas Young and French Egyptologist Jean-Francois Champollion.

MUSINGS

1. One group of hieroglyphics found on the Rosetta Stone was enclosed in an oval called a cartouche. Think of five symbols that would represent your personality and create a personal cartouche.

2. Hieroglyphics are symbols representing objects and ideas. They may be the oldest form of writing. Find out what some of these symbols are, and use them to create your own message. Draw them on paper, cardboard, wood, etc. Add color and display them in the library, where other students may enjoy them.

MENTAL MIXTURES

Find and examine samples of two or three ancient languages. How are they alike? How are they different? Summarize your observations and create a poster display.

MOVING BEYOND
Codices
Cuneiform
Egyptian Kings
Egyptology
Obelisk
Pictographs

The Sphinx

Near the Cheops Pyramid of Giza, Egypt, is one of the most famous of Egyptian monuments, the Sphinx. The figure is that of a reclining lion with the face of a man. Built around 2250 B.C., it is 240 feet in length and carved out of limestone blocks, about three times larger than those used to construct the Pyramid. Scientists believe that the statue was intended to be a symbol of Egyptian royalty, since the name Sphinx comes from the Egyptian word *seshepanky*, or living image. This strange image was also used in countries bordering Egypt.

The famous "riddle of the Sphinx" evolved in 1600 B.C. under the name of Hamarchis who posed this riddle: "What speaks with one voice, yet goes on four legs, then two, then three?" According to legend, it means: "Man is the answer, for he crawls on four legs as a child, goes on two as an adult, and walks on three, his own plus a cane, when old." It will be a riddle for generations to come!

MUSINGS

1. Step into a "time-machine" and go back to the time of the building of the Sphinx. Think about five questions you would like to ask the builders and write them down with possible answers they might give.

2. Create an original riddle about the Sphinx. Try it out on classmates or family members.

MENTAL MIXTURES

Theories about the purpose of the Sphinx are that it was connected to the Pyramid of Cheops and was used for its secret chambers and passageways during mummification. It was a way to protect the last preparations of the king and all of the treasures with which he would be entombed. Examine pictures of the proximity of the Great Pyramid and the Sphinx. Make an underground sketch showing how they might have been connected and used.

MOVING BEYOND

Anubis	Canopic Jars	Codes
Isis	Osiris	Riddles

Stonehenge

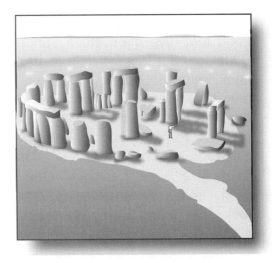

The lonely Salisbury Plain in the south of England holds one of the world's greatest mysteries—Stonehenge. Dating back over 4,000 years, this construction of gigantic stones awes all who see it.

The first accurate charting of Stonehenge was in the 1870s. The great cluster of huge stones had a pattern of distinct circles and formations. Some of the stones are thought to have come from the Prescelly Mountains over 140 miles away. Scientists believe the structure is the result of several building stages during a 300-year period and could have been completed a thousand years *after* the building of the Egyptian pyramids.

Astronomers believe that it might have been used to calculate solar and lunar movements. On certain days of the year, the summer and winter solstices can be seen between the huge arches. It is the path of the sun when its distance from the equator is the greatest. The solstices occur each year around June 22 and December 22.

Many questions need answers. How did ancient people transport the huge monolithic stones from mountains to plains? What system was used to set the top stones of each arch? Why was such a structure needed? The questions continue; the answers are vague.

MUSINGS

1. Huge structures abound from ancient times. Set up a chart to compare Stonehenge, the Great Pyramid, and the Great Wall of China. Compare their possible purposes, dates constructed, and outstanding features.

2. Using a constellation chart, find the star formations for the summer and winter solstices. Use a sheet of black art paper and lightly draw these with white crayon or paint. Use a straight pin to poke through the paper at the place where the main stars of constellations are located. Label each of these. When complete, hold the paper up to a window or an indoor light to see the stars "shining."

MENTAL MIXTURES

Explain why you think this ancient group of builders felt the need to so precisely place certain stones at the Stonehenge site. Prepare a short "scientific" paper defending your views.

MOVING BEYOND

Angkor Wat	Ephesus	Pharos of Alexandria
Persepolis	Roman Catacombs	Temple of Diana

Stone Spheres

During the summer of 1967 at an elevation of 6,000 feet, five giant stone spheres were discovered in Mexico. Six to eight feet in height, they resembled other stones found in Costa Rica. Weighing about 12 tons, they are smoothly finished and almost perfectly rounded. They are made of soft volcanic rock placed in rows and formal groupings. Hundreds were also found in the surrounding areas.

After careful scientific study, it was determined that the spheres were probably formed during the Tertiary geological period, many years ago. High temperatures of 1,000 to 4,000 degrees Fahrenheit and slow cooling was the process that formed these giant relics. As if flung by a huge hand, they littered the landscape by the hundreds in many areas. Similar spheres dot the landscape throughout Mexico and in areas near Los Alamos, New Mexico.

Is there a relation between these spheres? Did early man use them? Was Mother Nature responsible? How did they become so widespread? Wonder and speculation abound about times long ago and the role the spheres might have played.

MUSINGS

1. Construct a time line showing the Tertiary Period and each era. Include significant events that occurred within each era.

2. What could be the reasons the stones were placed in certain groupings? Set up a list of possible ideas.

3. El Caraco is a great domed structure of the Mayas. It is also known as "the snail." Find out about this unusual site by writing a newspaper article describing what it is and where it is located. Add a sketch of the site and create an interesting headline.

MENTAL MIXTURES

Describe some uses for the giant stone spheres, as if you were living during that time. Illustrate your ideas showing these possible uses.

MOVING BEYOND

Ethnology   Geophysics   Speleology
U.S. Geological Survey   Volcanology

Tunguska

At 7 A.M. on June 30, 1908, above the Tunguska River Valley in Siberia, Russia, something moved across the sky from southeast to northwest. It looked like a pipe with a strange bluish glow around it, just before a tremendous roar was heard. Seconds later, the object shattered in a rapid series of explosions. Trees were knocked down in a pattern radiating from the epicenter in an area of over 2,150 square kilometers. At the epicenter of the explosion, the forest fires lasted for five weeks, destroying an area of 1,000 square kilometers. Buildings more than 600 kilometers away folded up from shock waves, and railroad tracks leapt into the air as the ground trembled and shook. So many tons of loose debris and dirt rose into the sky that a black rain fell for a week. The huge dust cloud caused the skies over Europe to turn white and yellow. Unusually colorful sunsets and sunrises and night skies bright enough to read a newspaper by were reported for weeks after the event.

Years later, the aftermath of the explosion still puzzles Russian scientists. They found trees knocked over, but no evidence of a meteoric crater. The speed of the object was calculated to be about 700 miles per hour. It was unlike other meteors that can travel about 100,000 miles per hour and leave round craters that travel in one direction. The mass of the object has been estimated at 100,000 tons, but no trace of asteroid material was found. It was estimated that the impact was equal to a 12-megaton bomb. Some scientists think the object may have been a comet, but no conclusive evidence of cosmic material has yet been found. The facts and evidence still exist, and so does the mystery!

MUSINGS

1. Create a diorama scene showing what might have taken place to cause this explosion.

2. In 1927, Leonid Kulik, a Russian scientist, was the first to mount an expedition to research the site. Find out what his conclusions were.

MENTAL MIXTURES

If you could set up an archaeological team to investigate the Tunguska site, what would be needed in the way of special team members, supplies, and equipment? Make a plan for the expedition. Remember that the Siberian winter temperature can fall to -70 degrees Fahrenheit!

MOVING BEYOND

Krakatoa	Mt. Etna	Mt. Vesuvius
Pompei	Siberia	Tundra

The Winchester House

A large Victorian-style house near San Jose, California, is probably one of the strangest homes in the world. After 38 years of complex and continuous construction activity, the house contains 10,000 windows, 40 bedrooms, 47 fireplaces, six kitchens, three elevators, 13 bathrooms, numerous secret panels and passages, steps leading nowhere, and doors that could be locked from the outside after entering.

The house held the private, secretive life of Sarah Winchester, wife of the famous William V. Winchester, maker of the Winchester Rifle, who died in 1888. Sarah was left an immense fortune of 30 million dollars along with a terrible fear of the ghosts of people slain by Winchester guns. Her house was a tribute to these "ghosts." Sarah bought the house and almost immediately hired a group of workmen to build the strange additions. She did this continuously for over 35 years.

No one knows why Sarah was so compelled to do this. She lived with only her butler and secretary; they were the only people allowed to see her.

MUSINGS

1. Write a letter to: The Winchester House, 525 S. Winchester Blvd., San Jose, CA 95128. Ask for free materials about this amazing place. Use them to create a poster display for a travel agent. Be sure to use the proper letter format!

2. Write up a real estate advertisement to sell the house. How could it be described?

MENTAL MIXTURES

The Winchester Model 1866 rifle came to be called "the gun that won the West." What did this mean? Explain your ideas.

MOVING BEYOND

The Alhambra, Spain

Biltmore Estate

Hearst Castle

The *House of the Seven Gables*

Imperial Palace, Tokyo

Victorian Architecture

44

Yonaguni Monument

Discovered in 1985 off the coast of Okinawa near the western coast of Japan, the undersea ruins near Yonaguni Island have created a brand-new mystery for scientists. The ruins around this new discovery are about 10,000 years old, including the length of time it took before the ruins sank into the water.

This underwater structure includes an unusual stepped pyramid estimated at over 150 feet in length by 65 feet in width. The top of the structure lies about 16 feet below sea level. There seem to be steps and platforms that range in size from $1\frac{1}{2}$ feet to several feet in height, resembling pyramidal structures found in Peru.

It has not been determined whether the ruins are man-made. If they are, they could be the remains of a culture not known about as yet. There are no records of a people advanced enough to have built this 10,000 years ago, yet the ruins still exist. This mystery, found in modern times, will provide years of exploration and speculation for archaeologists, anthropologists, and oceanographers alike!

MUSINGS

1. Draw a map of Japan and show the location of Yonaguni and Okinawa. Include a scale of miles and a compass rose.

2. Yonaguni predates the earliest-known structures in Japan by 5,000 years. Find out about the geological time period the ruins represent. What living things were present on Earth? What plant life was present? Name the era and draw some of the items that existed at that time.

3. The problems associated with investigating this underwater site are many. Make a list of all the things that could hamper exploration. Are there alternatives? What are they?

MENTAL MIXTURES

Using clay and scrap materials, construct a model of what Yonaguni might look like. Find pictures of it on the Web or in a recent encyclopedia. What tools might have been used as an aid to construction so long ago? Pretend that you lived 10,000 years ago and draw the kinds of tools and equipment that could have been made from materials in that natural environment.

MOVING BEYOND

The Blue Grotto	Jacques Cousteau	Marine Biology
Mu and Lemura	Oceanography	SCUBA

Summarizing

According to legends, the Atlanteans migrated to other continents to avoid the impending disasters that were coming. They brought their advanced knowledge with them to begin new colonies. The legends are enhanced by evidence of many similarities that exist today.

Before the voyages of Columbus, there were no known connections to suggest a link between many of the ancient countries, certainly none between Egypt, Mexico, or Central and South America. However, after the discovery of advanced civilizations in the New World, many similarities have been found.

Common features of civilizations include architectural style and advanced construction ability in the pyramids, with many aligned to cardinal points; similarities of myths and legends having to do with the gods of corn and sun; the use of devices to measure the seasons; calendars; and number systems. Many structures were built with megalithic stones containing extremely fine joint sections and L-shaped corners. Mummification was a process used by various cultures to honor the dead before burial.

There are great similarities between pictographs and hieroglyphic symbols. Each group had recorded histories worked out in stone or painted on interior walls. Easter Island can be aligned along a line that includes the Nazca Plains and the Great Pyramid.

Are there more similarities? Spend time comparing some of the mystery sites by identifying their map locations, structural types, likenesses, and differences. Summarize your thoughts in a concluding activity. Would any make an interesting place to visit? Which would you choose?

There are many other places of mystery; perhaps others can be added to this collection. Most of all—study, think, hypothesize, and enjoy!